You Must Be Joking!

You Must Be Joking!

Compiled and Illustrated
by Paul Brewer

Foreword by Kathleen Krull

Lots of Cool Jokes

Cricket Books

Chicago

Library of Congress Cataloging-in-Publication Data
Brewer, Paul.
  You must be joking : lots of cool jokes / compiled and illustrated by
Paul Brewer with an introduction by Kathleen Krull.— 1st ed.
      p. cm.
Summary: A collection of over two hundred jokes and riddles, grouped by
subject, plus tips on writing, learning, and telling jokes.
  ISBN 0-8126-2661-3 (pbk. : alk. paper)
  1. Wit and humor, Juvenile. [1. Jokes. 2. Riddles.] I. Title.
  PN6163.B744 2003
  818'.5402—dc21

                                                        2002013926

For Judy O'Malley

Knock, knock.
Who's there?
Jo King.
Jo King who?
You must be Jo King!

Contents

Foreword

Sometimes I'll be talking to Paul . . . and he's not listening. His eyes glaze over. They remind me of two Krispy Kreme doughnuts. I know what's coming: OH NO, IT'S ANOTHER JOKE!

Seconds later, out of his mouth it comes. Sometimes it's lame, and I groan. Or gross, and then I gag.

But sometimes it's perfect—such a surprise twist on whatever's going on that I burst out laughing. Occasionally, I hoot or chortle, or even scream the highest of compliments: "You're killin' me, Brewer!" (For a joke-teller, any response is a good response.)

Paul then goes back to listening to me, or whatever he's supposed to be doing. He's happier, and more often than not, I am, too.

Being someone who compulsively makes up jokes—even writes books about them—has its ups and downs. Being the wife of such a person has its own challenges. . . .

Oops, I've run out of space—plus it's time for some jokes. Luckily for me, I believe that nothing in life is more important than a sense of humor. May jokes fill your own lives—starting with these!

—*Kathleen Krull*

Acknowledgments

I would like to thank Judy O'Malley, Tony Jacobson, Heather Delabre, Marc Aronson, Susan Cohen, and Janice Brookes. Thanks also go to all my friends who lent their support and occasionally some jokes. Special thanks go to my wife, Kathy Krull, for all her assistance in helping me polish this thing up. And final thanks to my brother Gary, his wife Aline, and their eight-year-old son Cyrus, who has called me many times to tell me another joke he has heard or made up. Cyrus is a great joke-teller!

Introduction

When I was a kid, one of my two favorite things was trying to be funny and, in particular, telling jokes. The other was drawing pictures (well, doodling to be exact). Now I get paid to do both. How cool is that?!

I recently read somewhere that kids laugh around 200 times a day. I'm pretty sure that I laughed at least that much when I was young. One of the many things that kept me laughing was telling jokes . . . all the time! When I first heard a joke, I couldn't wait to run off and tell my friends. And that would start it: we'd sit around sharing our jokes and giggling hysterically, easily reaching that goal of laughing 200 times!

I think I was around twelve or thirteen when I got a tape recorder for my birthday. I used it—almost entirely—to tape everything that was funny to me. I would tape myself or my friends telling jokes or just plain being silly. Sometimes I'd record the commercials on TV, then my friends and I would goof around, changing the product's name by recording over it with something wacky and funny that we dreamed up. Turning the recording into the form of a joke was the goal. We'd then play it back over and over again and laugh our heads off at what we came up with. We thought we were geniuses!

Nowadays, I collect joke books so that I can find the best jokes to go into a book like this. In one of our bathrooms we have a bookcase full of nothing but books of humor. I have developed a sort of internal joke-o-meter that comes in handy when choosing the jokes I like and want to retell in my own way. For this book, I looked at thousands of jokes. Some made it, but a whole bunch didn't. Jokes are personal. Some jokes that made my wife fall on the floor laughing didn't get into this book. But hey, it's my book.

I am constantly in search of all things funny. They can be in the form of books, magazines, or newspapers with hilarious stories, articles, pictures, or cartoons. I love funny movies and TV shows, the Internet is absolutely loaded with humor, and I always bust up over funny greeting cards. Gross, silly situations (and you all know what I'm talking about) still have me on the floor in stitches.

I don't tell as many jokes now as I did when I was young. But when I'm with people, I do try to find the humor in situations around us and make fun out of what I see and hear. These are the "you-had-to-be-there" jokes; they're funny only in the situation. Sometimes *very* funny. Getting other people—and of course myself—laughing is the goal because laughter almost always makes for a good time!

Humor is important in life; it can help you through the tough times. If I'm feeling down, one of the best ways that I know of to come out of it is with laughter. It is a scientific fact that laughing releases endorphins, a chemical in the body that makes you feel good. Laughing is a great way to reduce stress. It's playtime for the brain. Many jokes actually rely on wordplay for their humor. Not to make jokes sound too "good for you," but they really do fire up the brain, develop your verbal skills (and your sense of humor), and give you practice speaking in front of other people.

Want to overcome shyness? Tell a joke. Don't know how to tell jokes? You've come to the right place—this joke book is also a "Why-to and How-to Book." Read the jokes and then check out the "17½ Tips for Remembering, Telling, and Making Up Your Own Jokes" at the end of the book. Whether you are brave or shy, jokes are a great way of getting attention, entertaining others (and yourself), making friends, or even distracting people who might want to beat you up.

At the end of this book, I give some tips about things like the setup, the timing and pacing of a joke, and building up to a surprise factor with the delivery of the punch line. I'll also throw in some tips on how to remember jokes, which is probably the hardest part about the whole joke-telling experience. And oh yeah—this book also includes a whole bunch of very funny jokes. In case that's still not enough to get you writing and telling your own jokes, at the end of each chapter I left a joke unfinished for you to complete. The suggested answers (you may come up with something different—or even better) are printed upside down on the bottoms of the pages. Last but not least, at the end of "17½ Tips," I give you a humorous illustration, and it will be your job to come up with the joke and punch line.

There are about 200 jokes in this book. If you find them all funny, you could reach that goal of laughing 200 times in a day. But why stop there? Add your own and set a new record. Go for 300!

It's a tough world out there, but life is funny and so are the jokes in this book. Turn the page. Start laughing!

—*Paul Brewer*
www.paulbrewer.com

UFOs
(Unidentified
Funny
Observations)

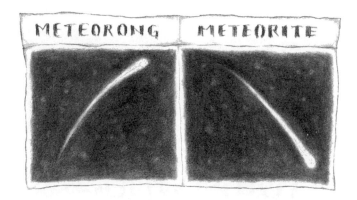

First Alien: Excuse me—is that the sun or the moon?

Second Alien: I don't know. I'm not from around here either.

Why did the Martian get a ticket?
He forgot to pay the parking meteor.

What did E.T.'s mom say when he got home?
"Where on Earth have you been?"

Pam: Did you ever notice that aliens have no noses?

Elliott: Really? How do they smell?

Pam: Oh, terrible.

First Alien: Is there a place around here where I can wash up?

Second Alien: Sure, just keep going straight ahead till you come to the meteor showers.

Two aliens landed their ship in Washington, D.C. After they exited their craft, the first thing they came upon was a fire hydrant.

"We are aliens from another planet, and we come in peace. Take us to your leader," said the first alien.

The second alien burst out laughing. "You're not going to get very far asking a little kid for help!"

How did the Martian wreck his spacecraft over and over again?
He kept driving into black holes.

Gorbot and Tobrog, two young aliens from another galaxy far, far away, landed next to a blinking traffic light.

"I think she likes me," said Gorbot.

"You're a space case," said Tobrog. "She's winking at me, not you!"

How can you tell if an alien has been using
    your toothbrush?
It glows in the dark.

Two aliens were zooming around the universe in their flying saucer, looking for a place to eat.

One said, "Let's go to the planet Earth's moon. There's a great restaurant there called the Lunar Café."

The other alien said, "I know that place— the food's O.K., but it's got no atmosphere."

Ned: Did you hear Dracula is starring in a
    new *Star Wars* movie?
Donna: Really? What's it called?
Ned: *The Vampire Strikes Back.*

How can you tell that an alien's been in your
closet?

All your hats are stretched out to twice their
size.

How does the universe hold up its pants?
With an asteroid belt.

What was Luke Skywalker's favorite restaurant?
Jabba the Pizza Hutt.

And where would you find a Jabba the Pizza Hutt?

At the Darth Mall.

How does Luke Skywalker get to the Darth Mall?

In his Toy-Yoda.

What did the ones say to the threes and fives?

"May the fours be with you."

What did everyone catch on board the *Enterprise*?

Answer: Chicken Spocks

Hairy and Scary

How many monsters does it take to screw in
a light bulb?
Twenty. One to do it, and nineteen to rebuild
the house.

What do you get when you cross a brilliant
man and a monster?
Frank Einstein.

What did the Hunchback of Notre Dame do
after he brushed his teeth?
He gargoyled.

Why was Dr. Frankenstein never lonely?
He could always *make* friends.

Which monster is safe to put in the washing
machine?
A wash-n-werewolf.

Ghost: I feel faint.
Doctor: You should—you're as white as a
sheet.

What kind of restaurant does Dracula hate?
A stake house.

What does Godzilla eat when he goes to a
restaurant?
The restaurant.

Why does Godzilla spew fire from his mouth
and stomp on cars?
His favorite food is toast and traffic jam.

Godzilla: I think we're getting close to the city.

Mrs. Godzilla: Why do you say that?

Godzilla: We're stepping on more people.

A skeleton walks into a juice bar.

"What would you like?" the clerk asks.

"Oh, just give me a smoothie and a mop,
    please."

Invisible Man: Did you miss me while I was
gone?
Invisible Man's Wife: Oh, were you gone?

Invisible Boy's Mother: Why are your grades
so terrible?
Invisible Boy: Because the teacher always
marks me absent.

First Cannibal: Am I late for dinner?
Second Cannibal: Yes, everybody's eaten.

Why did the Blob eat the North Pole?
He wanted a frozen dinner.

Ms. Monster: Sometimes I don't think you
have a brain in your head!
Mr. Monster: Which head?

First Zombie: Wow, your child is so big.
Second Zombie: Yes, he gruesome.

What do you call a witch who likes to go to
the beach and lie around, but is afraid
to go in the water?
A chicken sand-witch.

What goes *Hahahaaaaaaaaah! Thump!*?

Answer: You, laughing your head off!

www.
YouMustBeJoking
.net

Why was the ghost's message so scary?
It sent an eeeeeee-mail.

Nick: Why don't you ever see fish using
computers?
Katie: I don't know. Why?
Nick: They're afraid of getting snagged
online and caught in the Net.

Quentin: Why on earth do you have jumper
cables hooked up to your computer?
Rashad: My crazy uncle is trying to restart it.

What do computers like to snack on?
Silicon chips, cookies, and spam, one byte at
a time.

Thomas: My silly mom just went to the store
to buy shoes for my computer.
Vicky: Why would she do that?
Thomas: I told her it needed to be rebooted.

How did the computer catch a cold?
Somebody opened too many Windows.

Bill Gates: Waiter, what's this spider doing in
my soup?
Waiter: I believe it's starting up a Web site.

Teacher: Isaac Newton discovered the law
of gravity when an Apple fell on his head.
Student: Ouch! Was that a desktop or a laptop?

Why did the woman take her computer to a
chiropractor?
To fix a slipped disk.

How can you tell if your parents have been
using your computer?
Wite-Out on the screen.

Why did the housekeeper refuse to clean the
computer?
She didn't do Windows.

How can you tell if a vampire is sending you
e-mail?
Your computer bytes you.

What did the laptop do when it went to the
beach?
It put on some screensaver and surfed the
Net.

**What do computers do when you tell them
a joke?**

Answer: They LOL

Movies, Music, and Other 'Musement

Why did Brahms take five years to compose
his famous lullaby?
It kept putting him to sleep.

Why did the composer never leave his bed?
He spent all his time writing sheet music.

Natalie: I once sang for the king of Freedonia.
Lucy: You're kidding.
Natalie: Well, that's what he told me. He said,
"If you're a singer, then I'm the king of
Freedonia."

"Will the band members play anything I ask
them to?" said the man at the Loud Rock Club.
"Sure," said the waitress.
"Well, could you ask them to play nothing?"

Piano Tuner: I'm here to tune your piano,
ma'am.
Mrs. Tonedeff: But I didn't call you.
Piano Tuner: No, but all your neighbors did.

Did you hear about the dweeb who got a
camera for his birthday?
He just picked up his first roll of developed
film—twenty-four photos of his right eye.

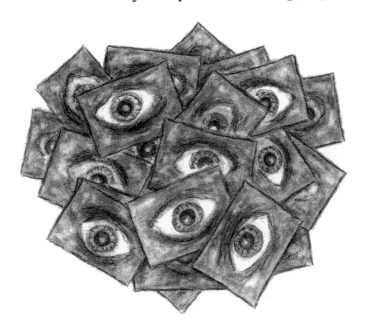

What happened to the composer who took
too many baths?
He started writing soap operas.

Why did the singer bring a pencil onstage?
He wanted to draw a big crowd.

Where do clowns go to college?
Har-Har-Har-Harvard.

Movie Attendant: Sir, this is the fifth ticket
you've purchased.
Customer: I know, but the girl in there keeps
tearing them up.

Felix: I used to be a tap dancer, but I had to
quit.
Hannah: Why?
Felix: I kept falling into the sink.

How does a Pokémon sneeze?
Pik-achu!

A man once invented a wooden car . . . but no
one would buy it because it wooden go.

A man goes to a lumberyard and asks for
some two-by-fours.

"How long do you need them?" asks the
yardman.

"Oh, for a really long time. I'm building a
house."

Did you hear about the dweeb who went to
the mind reader?
He only got charged half price.

Paulino: Mom, I was playing my harmonica,
and I swallowed it!
Mom: Good thing you weren't playing a tuba!

What did Hamlet say at the Weight Watchers
meeting?
"Tubby or not tubby?"

A man called an airline office in San Diego and asked, "How long does it take to fly to Chicago?"

"Just a minute," said a voice on the other end.

"Wow! That's not very long. Thanks!" said the man, and he hung up.

What do joke-tellers have for breakfast?

Mayhem, Mishaps, and Miscellaneous Madness

A woman once stole a calendar and got twelve months.

What did the old Egyptian get by staring at the river?
See-Nile.

Becki: What kind of underwear is useful at a fire?
Emily: I don't know. What kind?
Becki: Panty-hose.

What would happen if a piano fell on you?
You would B-flat.

First Robber: Oh no, it's the cops! Jump out the window!

Second Robber: You must be joking—we're on the thirteenth floor!

First Robber: Just do it! This is no time to be superstitious.

Doctor: I have some pretty bad news to tell you. You have only twenty-four hours to live.

Patient: You must be kidding, Doctor.

Doctor: No, I'm not, and it gets worse. I forgot to tell you yesterday.

A woman calls the fire department to report that her garage is on fire.

"How do we get there?" asks the dispatcher.

The woman says, "Oh, don't you guys use those big red trucks anymore?"

Convict's Wife: It's too bad you went on a hunger strike.

Convict: Why is that?

Convict's Wife: I put a file in your cake.

Inmate #072952: What are you in for?

Inmate #101450: Driving too slow.

Inmate #072952: Huh? Don't you mean too fast?

Inmate #101450: No, I mean too slow. The cops caught me.

First Scientist: Hey, check it out! I just made one comedian out of another.

Second Scientist: Oh, would you stop cloning around!

Judge: You broke into the same shoe store three nights in a row—why?

Robber: Well, the first pair was too big, and the second pair was too small, but the third pair fit just right.

Why did the lawyer leave the courtroom in his underwear?

He lost his law-suit.

Paramedic: Where are you hurt?

Accident Victim: I don't know—I haven't seen my lawyer yet.

What would happen if you flushed yourself down the toilet?

You'd be committing sewer-cide.

Store Employee: A guy just ran out of the store with two jackets, three sweaters, and a pair of pants.

Store Manager: Why didn't you go after him?

Store Employee: They were my pants!

First Prisoner: What are you in for?

Second Prisoner: For stealing a pig.

First Prisoner: Oh yeah? How did they catch you?

Second Prisoner: The pig squealed.

A woman is driving down the freeway, knitting at the same time. A policeman notices this, drives up alongside her, and shouts, "Pull over!"

"No!" she yells back. "It's a scarf!"

Copilot: Sir, we're now going faster than the
speed of sound!
Pilot: What?

What happened to the man who ran away
with the circus?
The police eventually caught up with him
and made him bring it back.

What was not served on the *Titanic*?

Answer: Life Savers and root beer floats

A Tasty Collection

Two hot dogs were cooking on the grill. One
said to the other, "It sure is hot in here."
The other hot dog screamed, "OH NO! IT'S A
TALKING HOT DOG!"

What kind of food takes you to court?
Sue-shi.

Did you hear about the man who ate yeast
and shoe polish each night before bed?
Every morning he would rise and shine!

Young Boy: Mom, this sandwich has Swiss
cheese on it. You know I don't like cheese
with holes!
Mother: Well, then just eat the cheese and
don't eat the holes.

Niki: Pablo, why are you staring at that can
of frozen orange juice?
Pablo: It says "concentrate."

Why can't two melons get married in a hurry?
Because they cant-elope.

What's the heaviest soup in the world?
Won-ton soup.

Mother: Eat your greens, honey. It'll put color
    in your cheeks.
Daughter: But, Mom, I don't want green cheeks!

What did the dweeb say when the waitress
    brought over a bowl of Cheerios?
"When did you start serving doughnut seeds?"

A young man on a business trip asks the hotel clerk for a restaurant recommendation.

"There's a great place around the corner that claims it can supply anything a customer orders," says the hotel clerk.

At around seven o'clock that evening, the young business traveler is seated at the restaurant, where, after careful consideration of the rarest of possible selections, he decides to order baked kangaroo on a bagel.

A few minutes later the waitress returns to say, "I'm so sorry, sir, but we are fresh out of bagels."

Customer: Waitress, I'd like a cup of coffee without cream, please.
Waitress: Oh, I'm sorry, but we're out of cream. Would you like it without milk?

Customer: Waitress, this fish is bad.
Waitress: You're a bad fish! Bad, bad, bad!

Customer: I'll have the lamb, please, and make it lean.
Waitress: Sure. To the right or to the left?

Customer: Waiter, I don't think I like this piece of bass. It's not half as good as the one I had here last week.

Waiter: Well, I don't understand why. It's from the same fish!

Customer: This chili tastes like dog food.

Waiter: Well, that's not possible. Cat food does not taste like dog food!

Customer: Waiter, my sandwich is talking to me!

Waiter: Didn't you order the tongue sandwich?

What does a cannibal order when he goes out to a restaurant?

Answer: The waiter.

I Will Not Tell Jokes in Class

Kathy came home from her first day at school.

Her mother asked, "Well, what did you learn today?"

"Not enough," Kathy replied. "They want me to come back tomorrow."

Teacher: Can anyone tell me what a forum is?
Amir: 2-um plus 2-um.

Teacher: Chynna, could you tell me what
n-e-w spells?
Chynna: New.
Teacher: That's right! Now tell me what
k-n-e-w spells.
Chynna: Canoe.

Teacher: Latoya, can you point out North
America on the map?
Latoya: It's right there!
Teacher: Good. O.K., class, who discovered
America?
Class: Latoya!

Teacher: Cyrus, let me see your homework
   assignment.
Cyrus: I can't. It blew away while I was walking
   to school.
Teacher: Really? And why were you late for
   school?
Cyrus: I had to wait for a strong wind.

Teacher: Monday you told me your homework blew away. Tuesday you said it got flushed down the toilet. Wednesday you said a burglar broke into your house and stole it. Thursday you said it dropped down the garbage disposal. Then I asked you to bring your parents to school today. So where are they?

Cyrus: Um . . . my dog ate them?

Teacher: Where's your pencil, Nick?

Nick: I ain't got one.

Teacher: No, no, Nick—where's your grammar?

Nick: She's at home, and she ain't got my pencil neither.

Teacher: Where is *your* pencil, Emily?

Emily: I ain't got a pencil.

Teacher: No, no, no! Repeat after me: I do not have a pencil, you do not have a pencil, they do not have a pencil. Do you understand?

Emily: No, not really. Where did all the pencils go?

Teacher: Here's a problem, Max. If you have
$5 in your front pocket, $10 in your back
pocket, and $25 in your wallet, what
would you have?

Max: Somebody else's pants.

Teacher: Frank, what do you call the outer
part of a tree?

Frank: I don't know.

Teacher: Bark, Frank, bark!

Frank: Arf! Arf!

Teacher: Your father's hair would turn gray overnight if he saw the way you've been acting up in class today.

Robert: Actually, he'd be very happy about that—he's bald.

Teacher: Does anyone know who invented fractions?

Judy: I think it was Henry the ⅛th.

Teacher: Calista, why do bears hibernate and sleep for six months?

Calista: Who would dare wake them up?

Teacher: Suzy, can you spell "wrong" for me?

Suzy: R-O-N-G.

Teacher: That's wrong!

Suzy: That's what you wanted, wasn't it?

Teacher: When I was your age, I could name all the presidents in order.

Jamar: When you were my age, there were only three of them.

Dad: How could you have failed that test?

Renee: Because of absence.

Dad: What do you mean? You were absent that day?

Renee: No. The girl who sits next to me was.

Teacher: Marty, could you tell me where the English Channel is?

Marty: I don't know, teacher. We don't have cable.

Teacher: Why are you eating your spelling test?

Maria: You told us it was a piece of cake.

Ms. Greer: Which is farther away—the moon
    or New Zealand?

Gary: New Zealand.

Ms. Greer: Why would you say that?

Gary: Well, I can see the moon, but I can't
    see New Zealand.

**Teacher: Paul, can you tell me what 52, 67,
and 78 are?**

**Answer:
Paul: That would be MTV, Comedy Central,
and Nickelodeon.**

Jokes That Jump

Why don't centipedes play soccer?
By the time they get all their shoes on, the
  game has ended.

Colin: Oh no! It's a run home!
Caitlin: Don't you mean a home run?
Colin: No, I mean run home. You hit the ball
  through the neighbors' window!

Angry Neighbor: Is this your ball, son?
Boy: Well, that depends.
Angry Neighbor: Look here, son, somebody
  just hit this ball through my window.
Boy: Well, then it's not mine.

What do you get when you cross a basketball
  player and a groundhog?
Six more weeks of basketball season.

Why was the baseball player sent to prison?
He had a hit-and-run, stole the bases, and got
  three strikes.

Why is basketball the grossest sport?
The players dribble all over the court.

Ahmet: Hey, have you ever hunted bear?

Elan: Nope, but I've gone fishing in my
underwear.

Coach: Zack, don't you know what a personal foul is?

Zack: Isn't it having your own chicken?

What did the cannibal say when a skateboarder rolled by?

"Oh, look—meals on wheels!"

Jean: Guess what—I went riding this afternoon.

Sheila: Horseback?

Jean: Sure is. He got back an hour before I did.

Becky: How did you hurt your arm?

Kevin: I was playing football with a candy machine.

Becky: What do you mean?

Kevin: I was trying to get my quarterback.

TV Reporter: So how long have you been running?

Track Star: Since I was around ten years old.

TV Reporter: Wow, you must be exhausted!

Sergio: My friend's father is a very rich man.
Aline: How rich is he?
Sergio: His son has a chauffeur-driven skate-
board.

Man in Uniform: Catch any fish this morning?

Freddy Fisherman: Did I ever! I caught over thirty fish.

Man in Uniform: Do you know who I am? I'm the game warden, and you've caught way over your legal limit.

Freddy Fisherman: Do you know who I am? I'm the biggest liar on the lake.

What's the difference between a boxer and a man with the flu?

One knows his blows, and the other blows his nose.

Mom: How did your first soccer game go, dear?

Debbie: It was all right, Mom, but those other girls never learned how to share.

Mom: What makes you say that?

Debbie: They were fighting the whole time over who gets the ball.

One morning, bright and early, a young man rents a deep-sea fishing boat and heads out for a day of fishing. His plan is to catch a bunch of fish and bring them home for dinner to surprise his wife. He spends all day at sea but has no luck at all. By the time the boat arrives back at the dock, he has caught absolutely nothing. On his way home he stops at a market that sells fresh fish. He asks the fish-seller to throw him two white sea bass, two albacore, and three halibut.

"Why do you want me to throw them to you?" asks the fish-seller.

The man responds, "I want to be able to tell my wife that I caught these fish!"

Why is it so hard to win at sports in the jungle?

Answer: Too many cheetahs

"Names 'R' Us"
by
I. M. Makenfun

Top-Ten Movie and Video Titles

The Haunted, starring Eve L. Wunn and Tara
    Fide

The Creature from Space, starring Anne Allie
    Enn

Grand Canyon Disaster, starring Eileen Dover
    and Phil Wright Tinn

The Gambler, starring Rollin D. Dice and "Big
    Jack" Potts

It Wasn't Me, starring Ima Knott Acrook

Hanging On by a Thread, starring Willy
Makeit and Betty Wont

Murder in the Cemetery, starring Doug A. Hole
and Trudy Body Inn

Crime Doesn't Pay, starring Colin D. Copps
and Hugh R. Busted

Best of World Wrestling, featuring Russell
Wethmey and I. Will Hurtchu

Dog's World, starring Chasan D. Carz and Bart
Ken Allott

Top-Ten Song Titles

Baby, Baby, I Apologize by Thayer Thorry

Rain Is Fallin' on My Head by Rufus Leeking
and Anita Newhouse

Sing Along with Me by Carrie O'Kee

I Stole Your Heart Away by Ruth Les Wunn

Peek-a-Boo by I. C. Hugh

Where Ya Going, Baby? by Wade A. Minitt

Why'd You Leave Me? by Watt S. Amada

Whatcha Thinking, Baby? by Howard I. Know

I Worship You, Baby by Will Neil Down

Why Ya Such a Fool? by Yuri Begidiot

Top-Ten Book Titles

How to Run a Service Station by Phillip
McCarr and Bud Aaron D. Tyre

Healthcare for Your Baby by Petey O'Trishan

150 Famous Lawsuits by Sue D. Utterguy

The Killer Is Out There by R. Hugh Next

How to Get to the Top by Ellie Vator

The Best Guide for Borrowing Money by
Lynne Mia Buck

Let's Have a Look at Your Brain by Sarah
Bellum

Breakfast: The Most Important Meal of the Day
by Hammond Ecks and Chris P. Bacon

Basic Art Instruction by Drew D. Picture

Conquering Bad Breath by Hal E. Tosis

Can you think of a name for the author of this book: *You Must Be Joking!* ?

Possible answers: Hope U. Arlaffin, Hugh R. Laffin, Hugh Musby Laffin

Family Members, Big and Small

Mom: Let's go shopping. I want to pick out some new clothes for school. We need to buy you clothes that will last.

Barbara: The ones you pick will last forever all right, because I'm never going to wear them!

Dad: Why is your baby brother crying?

Tony: I wouldn't share my piece of cherry pie.

Dad: What happened to his piece?

Tony: Oh, he cried when I ate that, too.

Jade: Dad, Courtney broke my new doll!

Dad: Oh no—how did she do that?

Jade: I hit her over the head with it!

Father: Hey, Jason, did you finish your home-work?

Jason: No, Dad, it's driving me crazy. I just can't figure it out—could you please do it for me?

Father: No, son, it wouldn't be right.

Jason: Could you give it a try anyway?

Monica: This morning I accidentally gave my dad soap flakes instead of cornflakes for breakfast.

Celine: Was he mad?

Monica: Mad? He was foaming at the mouth!

Mom: Elana, these cookies taste terrible! Are you sure you just put in a dash of salt?

Elana: A dash of salt? Oh, no. I thought you said a dish of salt.

Melanie and her sister Jacqui sat down to eat a sandwich. Melanie cut the sandwich into two unequal pieces, took the large one, and gave the small one to Jacqui.

"You're so rude," said Jacqui. "If I'd cut the sandwich that way, I'd have taken the small piece and left you the large one."

"Then everything's O.K.," said Melanie. "You've got it."

Peggy: You won't believe this, but my parents let my crazy aunt name my new twin brother and sister.

Libby: So what did she name them?

Peggy: Denise and Denephew.

Mom: That's an unusual pair of socks you've got on, Desiree. One is pink with black polka dots, and the other is red with green stripes.

Desiree: Yeah, I know, Mom. And what's really strange is that I've got another pair just like it upstairs.

Mary: Are worms good to eat, Dad?

Dad: Yuck, are you kidding? Why?

Mary: Because there was one in your salad.

The neighbor stared in shock at the boy pounding nails into the expensive maple furniture.

He turned to his host. "How can you afford to let your son do that to the furniture?" he asked.

"Oh, it's no problem—I get the nails cheap."

After a bad storm, three brothers in their small boat become shipwrecked on an uninhabited island in the middle of the ocean. No one comes to their rescue, so they must build themselves shelter and learn to live off the land. Several years pass, and one day the three of them find a magic lantern while walking down the beach. They pick it up and brush it off. Instantly, a genie appears.

"I have the power to grant three wishes— what will they be?" says the genie.

The brothers talk it over and decide they will each take one wish. The first brother says, "I want to go back home." He instantly disappears, sent back to his home.

"I want to go back home, too," says the second brother. He disappears and is on his way back home.

Now, the third brother was not the bright one of the bunch. Realizing that he is now all by himself, he says to the genie, "Please bring back my two brothers so I'm not alone!"

What did the dweeb say when his brother called him on his cell phone?

Answer: "How did you know I was at this store?"

Open Your Mouth and Say "Ha"

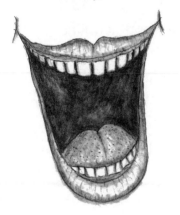

Doctor: Well, hello, Mr. Hill! I haven't seen you in quite a while.

Mr. Hill: I know, Dr. Keefe, I've been sick.

Doctor: Could you please breathe in and out for me three times?

Patient: Is that so you can check my lungs?

Doctor: No, I just need to clean my glasses.

Patient: Doctor, you gotta give me something for my headache!

Doctor: Well, I'm not too fond of headaches, but how about a dollar?

Patient: Doctor, one night I dreamed I was a tepee and the next night, a wigwam. What is my problem?

Doctor: I think you're too tents.

What did the judge say to the dentist?

"Pull my tooth, the whole tooth, and nothing but the tooth!"

Where did King Tut go to cure his back pain?

To the Cairo-practor.

Patient: Doctor, Doctor, my foot falls asleep
   every night.
Doctor: Well, what's wrong with that?
Patient: It snores, too!

Patient: Doctor, Doctor, my foot still falls asleep!
Doctor: Well then, try wearing loud socks.

A patient complaining of pain is admitted to the hospital. After many tests, the doctor recommends surgery and removes a tumor the size of a golf ball.

The next morning, the attending nurse says, "Mr. Krull, that was a serious operation you had. You are one very lucky man!"

Mr. Krull responds, "Oh yes, and I'd really like to thank the doctor. Could you get her for me?"

The nurse says, "No, I'm sorry, she's not in today. She's out playing golf."

Patient: Doctor, I broke my arm in two places!
Doctor: Well, don't go back to those two places again.

Patient: Doctor, I have a weak back.
Doctor: Oh really? When did you start to notice it?
Patient: About a week back.

Patient: I've been having this dream that I'm in a Laundromat, trapped inside a washing machine.

Doctor: What do you do?

Patient: I toss and turn.

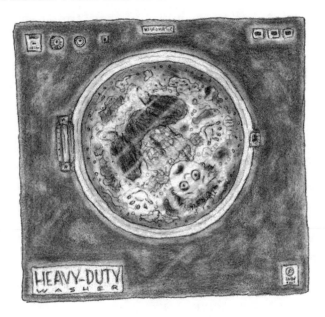

Patient: I have a problem, Doctor. I keep thinking that I'm a dog.

Psychiatrist: Well, have a seat here on the couch, and we'll talk about it.

Patient: But I'm not allowed on the couch.

"Doctor, Doctor, my son just swallowed some quarters, dimes, nickels, and pennies. Can you please help him?"

"Absolutely," said the doctor. "Let's just bring him in the examination room and have a look." About a half-hour goes by, and the doctor finally comes out.

"How is my son?" says the frantic mother.

The doctor replies, "There's no change yet!"

Mrs. Horschke goes to the eye doctor, complaining that she sees fuzzy spots all the time. She is checked by the doctor and given special glasses for her condition. A week later the doctor calls her at home to see how her eyes are doing.

"Oh, I can see the spots much better now!" replies the woman.

Patient: Doctor, I keep seeing cartoon characters, big as life, talking to me, just like I'm talking to you. What do you make of it?

**Answer:
Doctor: Sounds like you're having
Disney spells.**

Goofy Creatures, Big and Small

A woman goes into a pet shop to buy a watch-dog.

The pet shop owner says, "I have only one. He's about 90 years old in human years, but he's trustworthy."

The woman says, "Ninety years old! Are you sure he would make a good watchdog?"

The pet shop owner says, "Oh, sure—if you hear any suspicious noises, just wake him up, and he'll bark!"

What do you call a very strange female deer? A weirdoe.

Damon: What do you call a deer with no eyes?
Zandra: I have no-eye-deer.

What do sardines and Houdini have in common?
They get stuffed into cans, are locked in, and
the key is left on the outside.

What do you get when you cross a hyena
with a parrot?
An animal that laughs at its own jokes.

Why was the dinosaur afraid to go back to
the library?
Its books were 60 million years overdue.

What did dinosaurs listen to?
Raptor music.

What did the buffalo say to his boy when he
    sent him off to college?
"Bison!"

Why can't elephants fly on airplanes?
Their trunks won't fit underneath the seat in
    front of them.

How do you buy a half-dozen elephants?
Ask for a six pack-a-derms.

Why do elephants wear sunglasses?
With all these jokes about them, they don't
    want to be recognized.

Why don't elephants like elephant jokes?
They think they're Dumbo.

What did the dachshund say when it won the
    dog show?
"I am the wiener!"

Vincent: My poodle chases everyone on a
    bicycle. What should I do?
Trina: Take his bicycle away.

A woman takes her dachshund to the veterinarian.

"What seems to be the problem?" asks the vet.

"My dog has a very high fever."

"I've got the perfect remedy—give him mustard, ketchup, onions, and relish."

"Are you crazy? Why would I do that?"

"Best thing for a hot dog!"

Young Skunk: Aw, come on, Mom! Why can't I have a chemistry set for my birthday?

Mother Skunk: Because it would stink up the house!

A snail is crawling down the sidewalk and gets mugged by two slugs. At the police station the sergeant asks him what happened.

"Well, I really can't recall very clearly," says the snail. "It all happened so fast."

What is your dog's favorite joke?
Eating stuff off the ground that is disgustingly gross, then licking your face.

One night a woman is sitting in her living room on the couch, reading her favorite book. She hears a very tiny tapping at her door, only to find, when she opens it, a huge snail on her doorstep.

"Oh, gross," she says. She reaches down, picks up the snail, and with great force hurls it way into her backyard.

About six months go by, and once again she's sitting in the living room and hears a tiny tapping at her door. She opens it, and there, in the same spot, is the same large snail. She picks it up and looks at it closely. To her amazement, she can hear a tiny voice coming from the snail, so she holds it right up to her ear. She listens carefully, and at that moment, the snail in its very tiny voice says, "What was that all about?"

Why can't the Three Bears get into their house?

Answer: Goldi-locks the door

It's So Obvious!

Jessica: Do you have holes in your underwear?
Kenny: Of course not.
Jessica: Then how did you get them on?

What did Geronimo say when he jumped out
   of a plane?
"Me-e-e-e-e-e-e-e-e-e-e-e-e-e-e-e-e-e-e-e!"

What do you call cheese that's not yours?
Nacho cheese.

Laura: If all your clothes were stolen, what
   would you come home in?
Janell: The dark.

Why did Robin Hood always steal money
   from the rich?
Because the poor didn't have any.

Paul: I heard a cool new joke the other day.
   Did I tell you yet?
Annelise: Is it funny?
Paul: It's hilarious.
Annelise: Then you didn't tell me.

Why do animals eat raw meat?
They don't know how to cook.

What do you have growing on your face
between your nose and chin?
Tulips.

Suzy: What is 5Q plus 5Q?
Gerry: 10Q.
Suzy: Oh, you're welcome!

Why do geese fly south for the winter?
Because they can't drive.

Melanie: I got my new hamster in Holland.
Jacqui: Oh yeah? Which city?
Melanie: Hamsterdam.

What would you catch if you fished with
    peanut butter?
Jellyfish.

Mr. Burnham: How many planets are in the sky?
Pat: All of them!

Teacher: How long did Cleopatra live?
Miles: All her life?

Teacher: When did Julius Caesar die?
Fiona: Just before he was buried.

Mel (on phone): You don't say! . . . Really? . . .
    You don't say? . . . You're kidding. . . . You
    don't say! . . . O.K., 'bye.
Jacqui: Who was that?
Mel: He didn't say.

Justin: Why are you putting lipstick on your
    forehead?
Katie: I'm trying to make up my mind.

Frederique: Pablo, I have to go to the store now to buy some toiletries.

Pablo: Toilet trees! I didn't know toilets grew on trees!

What did the hair stylist say when the
customer asked to have a haircut?

Answer: "Sure, which one?"

Riddles

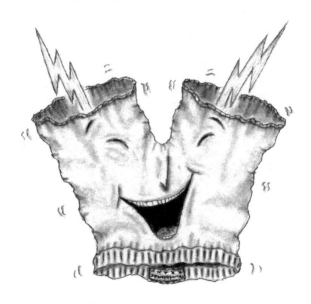

What do you call a quick American sketch?
A Yankee Doodle.

Why was 6 afraid of 7?
Because 7-8-9.

What do you call a dinosaur that knows all
the words?
A thesaurus.

How do you make a tissue dance?
Put a little boogie in it!

What did Rip Van Winkle say when his wife
woke him up after twenty years of sleep?
"Please, just five more minutes, dear."

Was there ever a period of history when
nerds ruled the world?
Yes—the Dork Ages.

What do you get when you cross a yellow
bear and a French dog?
Winnie-the-Poodle.

What kind of coffee do young cows drink?
De-calf.

How do you make anti-freeze?
Take away her jacket.

Why did the toilet paper roll down the hill?
To get to the bottom.

What do you call a hippie's wife?
Mississippi.

What do clouds have on when it's raining?
Thunderwear.

What do George Washington, Abraham Lincoln,
    and Martin Luther King Jr. have in common?
They were all born on holidays.

Why did the fireman always bring his dog to
    the fire?
To find the fire hydrant.

Who invented steak?
Sir Loin.

**What did the big booger say to
the little booger?**

Answer: "Don't get snotty with me!"

Knock, Knock

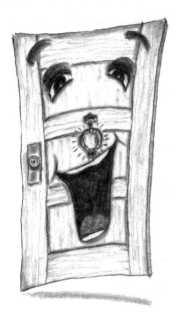

Knock, knock.
Who's there?
Who-who.
Who-who who?
I haven't even told the joke, and you're
laughing already!

Knock, knock.
Who's there?
Shirley.
Shirley who?
Shirley you know who this is!

Knock, knock.
Who's there?
Leggo.
Leggo who?
Leggo the doorknob and let me in!

Knock, knock.
Who's there?
Howie.
Howie who?
I'm fine, how are you?

Knock, knock.

Who's there?

Hoover.

Hoover who?

Hoover you expecting—a vacuum cleaner?

Knock, knock.
Who's there?
Yoda.
Yoda who?
Yoda weirdest person I know!

Knock, knock.
Who's there?
Topeka.
Topeka who?
Why do you like Topeka your nose?

Knock, knock.
Who's there?
Little old lady.
Little old lady who?
I didn't know you knew how to yodel.

Knock, knock.
Who's there?
Kid Jamaica.
Kid Jamaica who?
Kid Jamaica me something to eat?

Knock, knock.
Who's there?
Pokémon.
Pokémon who?
Pokémon in the eye, and he might poke you
    back!

Knock, knock.
Who's there?
Babylon.
Babylon who?
Babylon—I'm not listening to you anyway.

Knock, knock.
Who's there?
My panther.
My panther who?
My panther falling down!

Knock, knock.
Who's there?
Havana.
Havana who?
Havana great time, wish you were here.

Knock, knock.
Who's there?
Althea.
Althea who?
Althea later, alligator.

Knock, knock.
Who's there?
Telly.
Telly who?

**Answer: Telly good joke and
crack yourself up!**

17½ Tips for Remembering, Telling, and Making Up Your Own Jokes

Don't you hate it when you hear a really good joke and the next day you try to tell it to someone and can't even remember how it goes? Or worse yet, you start telling the joke, and you mess up the punch line?

You're not the only one! Most people have these problems. Learning how to tell jokes is a little like learning a foreign language. For example, in a new language you have to know the proper order of the words in a sentence to convey your exact meaning so that you don't end up saying something like, "I love you, banana," when you meant to say, "I really like bananas."

The same goes for a joke. If you tell it out of order, you might end up giving the punch line first and ruining the joke. Following a few basic rules will help you to remember and then tell your jokes for full comic effect. Also included are some simple tips on how to create your own jokes.

1. First of all, you have to *want* to tell jokes. (Making people laugh is a lot of fun!) It helps to tell the jokes you like the most. The funnier

you think a joke is, the more likely it is to stick in your brain.

2. Start with easy-to-remember jokes, such as riddles and knock-knocks. The predictable pattern of these jokes helps you remember the lines in the right order. When you feel comfortable telling simple jokes, try the longer ones. The ones that are hardest to remember are a bit like short stories, with several characters and situations. Memorize your jokes in groups: riddles, knock-knocks, story jokes. Then try to remember them by subject or type, like monsters, food, UFOs, sports, gross jokes, and so on. The jokes in this book are organized by topic and types of jokes, so pick your favorites from these as a starting collection.

3. Try to visualize the joke as a picture. For example,

What does Moby Dick eat for dinner?
Fish and ships!

What do you see? The ocean with the *whale* swimming, mouth open, toward *fish* jumping out of the water and *ships* floating along toward their certain fate—to be gobbled up.

What are the joke's key words?
  Moby Dick + fish + ships

Try memorizing just these key words instead of the whole joke. When you want to tell the joke, think "whale + fish + ships." Your brain will remember the rest, and you'll be able to tell it in the right order.

4. When you hear a good joke, write it down. Start a "Jokes" journal, or create a "Jokes" file on your computer. Organize by types (riddles, etc.) and subjects (sports, etc.).

5. There are a gazillion jokes that can be heard and found everywhere—way too many to remember. So don't try to cram a whole bunch of jokes into your head or you'll start to mix them up. Just start out learning your favorites. It's better to tell a few jokes really well than to try and learn every joke that you hear.

6. Practice, practice, practice till you get it right. A good place is in front of the bathroom mirror. Many famous actors and comedians have practiced in front of a mirror, so it's not as weird as it sounds. Act out the joke—make faces, move your hands. You can pretend the mirror is another person. When you start laughing, they start laughing. It helps you feel confident in telling the joke when you know your joke well before you try it out on someone else. Lots of practice will give you that confidence.

7. Try your jokes out on your friends, brothers and sisters, mom and dad—as many different people as you can. The more you tell a joke, the less likely you are to forget it and the more you'll feel sure that other people think it's funny.

8. Don't start out by saying you don't know how to tell jokes well. If you start to mess up a joke, keep moving. Don't apologize. Just stop, then start over, or move on to another joke. You can always go back later to the one you got stuck on.

9. Pace yourself—speak slowly and clearly. Don't blurt the lines out, or no one will understand. Try not to giggle when you tell a good joke. It's hard to understand you when you're laughing uncontrollably, and your laughter can spoil the surprise of a well-timed punch line.

10. When other kids have jokes to tell, listen closely. You might learn a hilarious new joke.

11. Making up your own jokes is not hard. A typical joke has two parts: a setup and a punch line. For example, in this riddle the setup is obvious—it's a question:

What's Godzilla's favorite sandwich? *(setup)*
Peanut butter and deli. *(punch line)*

The punch line will often answer the question in an outrageously different way than you might expect. In this case, peanut butter and jelly is a common sandwich, but Godzilla is a giant monster that eats everything. He would eat the entire deli (short for delicatessen, where sandwiches are made), which rhymes with "jelly."

12. The more fun you have playing around with the sounds and meanings of words, the funnier your jokes will be. List sounds and words that are fun to say and make you giggle (oodles, noodles, poodles, etc.) and make up jokes that use them in the punch lines. Write down words and see what they have in common, and use this as a seed to grow a riddle or a joke. For example:

Alien + surfing + galaxy = a joke.

Q: Where do aliens surf?

A: In the galax-sea.

13. Knock-knock jokes are pretty easy to make up. Start with a name that sounds like the beginning of a sentence. For example, the

name "Isadore" sounds like "Is the door . . ."
Finish up this knock-knock with whatever you
think sounds funny, and it might go something
like this:

> Knock, knock.
> *Who's there?*
> Isadore.
> *Isadore who?*
> Isadore unlocked? I want in!

14. Be aware of the timing of your joke.
Short is good, especially for punch lines. While
you're practicing and acting out your joke,
take out unnecessary words—get straight to
the point.

15. To get even more ideas, read other
joke books and substitute your own characters and situations—recycling is an easy way
to make jokes your own. (Hint: Riddles and
knock-knocks work best here.) For example:

> Q: What do you call a one-day-old cat in
> Alaska?
> A: A kitten.

This riddle is a good example of how easy it is

to recycle a joke. The possibilities are endless. You could change this to:

Q: What do you call a one-day-old dog in Toledo?

A: A puppy.

Or:

Q: What do you call a one-day-old cow in Calistoga?

A: A calf.

16. Some jokes involve real people and can sometimes be very funny. But be careful not to tell jokes that will hurt other people's feelings. You want to laugh *with* people, not at them.

17. If you really enjoy cracking yourself up and making your friends crack up, you'll do fine as a joke-teller. When you find your joke funny, other people will laugh, too. Say "Thanks!" when people tell you that your jokes are great.

17½. This last tip is just an illustration in need of a joke to describe it. I created it so that several different jokes could work well. See what you come up with—and have fun!

Remember, no matter how
you tell a joke, if it makes
someone laugh,
YOU MUST BE JOKING!

Is your funnybone hungry
for more?
Does your sniffer crave
bigger giggle-snorts?

Then check out
www.youmustbejoking.net
for more outrageously
hilarious jokes
by Paul Brewer!